Freedom
JOURNEYS

Real People. Real Stories.

Published by Kainon Land Media - Pace, Florida

www.KainonLandMedia.com

www.jenalowry.com

Printed in the United States of America

ISBN: 979–8–9870072–4–2

Title: Freedom Journeys. Real People. Real Stories.

Stories were collected and compiled by: Jena' Lowry

Scripture quotations are from the KJV King James Version, the ISV International Standard Version, the NHEB the New Heart English Bible, and the LOGOS version.

Edited by: Katie Cook, Dayna Hood, and Arian Cook

Cover design by: Katie Cook, and Arian Cook

Interior graphic designs by: Arian Cook and Jena' Lowry

Photography by: Jena' Lowry

Acknowledgments

Our intention and purpose for collecting these stories
is to ILLUMINATE the power of the Holy Spirit.
To enlighten all readers that GOD IS ABLE,
and we are not alone. To CELEBRATE what HE HAS
DONE in us! We want to thank every person who so
beautifully shared their journey with us. Without your
bravery, and your passion to see others FREE, there
would be no book. Thank you for allowing the Holy Spirit
to use you. To every reader, God loves you! You are
His. Wherever you are in life, God will meet you right
where you are. He stands at the door and knocks…

"As many as I love, I rebuke and discipline.
Be sincere therefore, and repent.
Behold, I stand at the door, and I am knocking.
If anyone hears My voice and opens the door,
then I will come in to him and I will dine with him,
and he with Me."
Revelation 3:19-20

"For The Son of Man has come to seek and to save
that which was lost."
Luke 19:10
-Jesus

Special Thanks to Ms Lyda. Thank you for being you!

Freedom Journeys:

There can be beauty in

Brokenness

The Beauty in Brokenness

Recently my oldest daughter and I walked the shores of our beach in search of shells. We were planning to use them for a project. As we walked, listening to the waves and absorbing God's Vitamin D, I noticed that she was picking up broken shells. "Not those. We can't use broken ones," I told her.

"I like these," she replied. "Of course she does," I told myself, "This is your child who always thinks outside the box." I knew that her part of the project would be more creative than mine. Later in the day, we agreed that I would be the one to take the shells home to wash and sort them.

This morning as I stood over the sink washing and sorting the shells, I noticed something. As I laid them down, broken from the unbroken, something caught my eye. I was drawn to the broken ones. There was something about them, that even though they had been broken, they still contained beauty.

Each having their own story.

Next to them were my unbroken shells, which as I added to their number began to look the same. It was as though their *appearance of perfection* had stolen their voice. They were lying there, silent. Nothing causing them to *stand out*.

Those who have come to know God, I mean really know Him, not just the name of God, but the character of God, will all agree that they came to Him BROKEN. Each with his own story, and yet, though broken, were lovingly and passionately accepted, repaired, and made WHOLE. Receiving their voice!

God doesn't require us to walk in the shame of the circumstances that caused our brokenness. Although, shame and guilt are products of past experiences, once REDEEMED, they should never become a strong hold in our future.

Instead, there's beauty in allowing brokenness to add to our voice; taking us to a place of CELEBRATION. A place of openly rejoicing over what God has done. To unashamedly, and freely, celebrate the FREEDOM in which He offered to us.

In 2 Samuel 16, King David danced! The Ark of the Covenant was a symbol of God's presence and glory. It had been lost, and forgotten about. But David sought to restore a place of worship for God's people, and when the moment arrived, David danced. He danced in celebration of its return because he understood the blessing associated with its presence. He became undignified as he celebrated. He removed his outward Kingly garments and exchanged them for a garment of humility.

God is a RESTORER, a HEALER, and a DEFENSE to those who call on Him. People deserve to know what He can do for them! If we keep quiet, if we allow shame and guilt (or even pride) to silence us, then where is the praise that God is so worthy of receiving.

3

In Mark 5:19,20... after Jesus set a possessed man free, He said to him, "Go to your house, to your own, and tell them what great things the Lord has done for you, and how He had mercy on you." And so he went his way, and began to proclaim in Decapolis how Jesus had done great things for him, and everyone was amazed.

These were people who knew the man. They had been aware of his bondage. Jesus knew they would celebrate with him, for what the Lord had done!

In Luke 17, Jesus entered a city. He was met by ten men who were lepers. They asked Jesus to have mercy on them. He replied, "Go and show yourselves to the priests." As they went, they were cleansed, (they had obeyed His direction). However, only one of them returned to glorify God. Only one used his voice to praise. Only one of them fell on his face at Jesus' feet, and gave Him thanks.

God deserves the glory! He deserves that we not hide His Goodness from others, but rather to be FREE to tell what He has done! Without Him, without His mercy, without His grace, we would have remained broken, alone, and void of true love.

Peter said these words... "Blessed be the God and Father of our Lord Jesus Christ, who according to His great mercy caused us to be born again to a living hope through the resurrection of Jesus Christ from the dead, to an incorruptible and undefiled inheritance that does not fade away, reserved in Heaven for you." -1 Peter 1:3,4

We should never forget our journey. Instead, it should remind us of who we were *before* Christ came and saved us. It should remind us of the Goodness and the Mercy of God, the God who loves us! It should remind us of where we never want to be again. It should create a heart of gratitude, and humility... that although we were once broken, He chose us. He called us out of the darkness, and into His light, and offered us an inheritance of LIFE!

I heard a loud voice
in Heaven, saying,
"Now has come the salvation,
the power,
and the Kingdom of our God,
and the authority of His Christ;
for the accuser of our brothers
has been thrown down,
who accuses them
before our God day and night.
They overcame him by the
BLOOD OF THE LAMB,
and by the word of their
TESTIMONY..."
Revelation 12:10,11

Jasmine's *Journey*

"I knew someone
was watching over me,
I just didn't know it was Jesus."

My biological father has never been a part of my life. When I was three my mom married, and at first, my stepfather appeared to be a "nice guy"... but we quickly realized that he was just the opposite.

He was abusive, both physically and sexually, to myself and my sister. The abuse continued from the age of three to the age of eleven. During this time, he and my mom had two children together.

It wasn't until my older brother reported the abuse to the police that it finally stopped. My stepfather was arrested, and my mom was charged with child-endangerment because of the things she had allowed him to do.

Shortly after, my mom took off taking my two younger siblings with her, choosing to abandon myself and my two older siblings.

Shortly after, we were sent to live with my grandmother, but by that time we had built barriers and walls due to the trauma. We trusted no one. We were hurt. We were angry. We felt alone.

WE WERE BROKEN.

After my mom left, I began searching. At the time, I didn't know what I was searching for.
Now, years later, I understand it was a search for love, and for acceptance.

Unfortunately, I found the unhealthy versions. I was looking in all of the wrong places, while running the streets.

At the age of thirteen, I remember my grandmother befriended a family. A man, his wife, and their three children. My grandmother wanted to help them.

The man took us places: fishing, to the store, and eventually... to his bed. At the age of fifteen, I found myself sleeping with a thirty-five-year-old man.

I hadn't been able to build boundaries for "self-protection" because unfortunately the abuse felt common. I was a child. Normally it's the job of adults to keep children safe. But for me, it hadn't been. So, by then, I had reached a place of not caring. Not caring what happened to me, or others. I was hurt.

By this age, drinking alcohol and smoking weed was a normal way to numb the pain. Eventually, I stole my grandmother's car and drove to New Orleans. There, I was taught to pick pockets and to steal. I did whatever it took to survive.

One day, after having to fight a man off of me, I left. I took a chance of returning to my grandmother, but instead was sent to a Wilderness program. However, I didn't go alone. Attached to me was a felony charge for grand theft auto.

After a year in the program, I still thought "my way" was the best way. I wasn't ready to submit to anything and I definitely wasn't taking "orders" from anyone. The only person I was trusting was ME!

Not long after my release I was introduced to cocaine. My list of trauma-induced pain had stacked up: anxiety, depression, and insecurities were building. At that time the avenue to drugs brought temporary relief.

Drug habits aren't cheap; so I found myself doing anything to supply it. Even if that meant sleeping with men, much older men. Whatever it took to NUMB THE PAIN.

At the age of seventeen, and after several unhealthy relationships, I met my son's father. He was twenty-seven and was the first person who showed me respect. It finally felt like someone actually cared for me.

At the age of eighteen, I had my son. I wasn't healthy. I had so many unresolved issues. So many broken places. So many voids I was trying to fill. Most of all, so much grief.

Stress mounted as it coincided with post-partum depression. By the time my son was five months old, someone introduced me to crack-cocaine for the first time... and I liked it. However, it led me on a completely different journey. Blinded by the illusion that it was providing needed relief, it was actually just the opposite.

One long night of using crack-cocaine, which I thought was being given to me for free, actually came with a price. With the rising of the sun, came a new pain. I was told that the drugs I had used that night were going to cost me and that I would have to work for them.

The sun came up, but I never went home. I was given clothes to wear, shown what to do, given instructions, and was sent out to the streets to stand on the corner. So, I did.

Not only did I become addicted to the drugs, but also to the lifestyle and the fast money. I honestly had never realized how many sick people there were, until being buried within that life. I was raped. I was beaten. I was kidnapped. Stomped in the head. Left for dead.

I've seen the ugliest side of people... and the ugliness of sin. Even through that, somehow, I knew someone was watching over me. I just didn't know it was Jesus.

At the time, I should have been dead. However, something... someone... was keeping me alive.

One morning, after being out on the streets all night, I found myself behind an abandoned building. It had been an extremely rough night. I was hungry. I was cold. I was tired. I remember saying these words: "God if you're really there, help me. I need you."

He heard me.

I was arrested. I like to think of it as being RESCUED. Rescued from being stuck in the lifestyle of prostitution. Through the arrest, God created a way out!

During a visit with the chaplain. I accepted Jesus as my Savior. Unfortunately, I wasn't ready to give Him my all.

I completed a year in a program. Which involved taking weekly and sometimes daily drug tests. I felt ready. I felt ready to try another way, instead of my way. I was determined. I felt the courage to keep going.

Yet, inside, I was still weak. I was trying to do everything through my own power, using my own strength... but it wasn't enough.
Something was missing.

Shortly after, I found myself in a relationship with a man in his fifties. However, looking back, I realize I was actually searching for the security of a Father. Even though this time, in this relationship, there was no direct physical abuse. He was a "player"... and I was empty.

I attempted, alone, to get my life together. I even registered for graphic design courses. However, the hunger inside, the pain, and the suffering never went away. It haunted me day and night. Until one day, after chasing empty things over and over...
I was arrested... again.

Even though the drugs provided only a TEMPORARY numbing of my pain, their hold was relentless.

Earlier that evening, a friend and I were doing drugs together. I was using a pipe and she was using a very unsanitary needle. After a while she began getting lumps on her body. I suggested that she go to a hospital, because I knew it was most likely a blood infection.

At first, she refused. I kept going, not slowing down on the pipe. I used to say, "I have a one crack mind" because at that time, drugs were controlling my will. Nothing else mattered.

A while later, I noticed the lumps were spreading over her entire body. I called the dealer and told him that if he didn't come and give her a ride to the hospital, he would be accountable if she died.

I went to the hospital with her. After she arrived, doctors quickly began giving her IVs to help with the infection.

However, even as I sat there watching my friend, the drugs were calling. They truly had a "strong hold", and I couldn't stop.

She knew I was continuing to go into the bathroom to do crack and she wanted some. After I refused, we began to argue. The hospital staff called security and I was asked to leave.

Drugs. Their bondage was so strong; it was impossible for me to break free, alone. There in the hospital, even facing the possibility of my friend dying, drugs were still calling.

I left the hospital and wandered around on the street. I was angry. Angry because my friend had turned on me. That's how things were out on the street. It wasn't a close community of friends caring for one another.

Instead, it was individual people trying to get what they wanted. At any cost. They would leave you with nothing and never think twice.

But GOD...

God in His mercy will reveal Himself right in the middle of your mess. Most would think that He would meet us in a church, at the foot of an altar, or in the presence of a minister. But God, because of His love for us, and because of the mercy He extends toward us, He is willing to meet us right where we are.

I was angry. I was hurt. I was lost. I was tired. I was tired of the life. I wanted out, but in my own strength I didn't know how. I didn't know how to break free.

Shortly after walking out of that hospital, a police officer approached me. He was different. Normally, the sight of a police officer brought fear, but this officer standing before me was different.

I remember he had red hair, green eyes, and a gentleness about him. It was as though he had an inner LIGHT. A light that I had never seen before. There was a presence... a peace that I had never felt before.

During our conversation, I lied to him about my name, about having drugs in my possession, and about having warrants. Lying to a police officer in itself is an offense, but that night there was something different.

A few moments later, during his questioning, I admitted to him that I had lied about my name and that I was sorry. He told me that he already knew, and for some reason he chose to extend grace.

Very wearily, I told him the truth and shared from my heart; "I'm tired," I told him. "I don't want to do this anymore. I'm just ready to lie down."

After looking up my real name he placed me in handcuffs, but this time was different. When I think about that moment, I can't help but get emotional. The presence that was there was one that I had never felt before. There was mercy and it was being extended to me. Undeserving mercy.

But isn't that just who God is?

Merciful.
Full of Grace.
Full of Unconditional Love.

Even though the drug charge was enough to send me to prison, that night the only charge against me was a V.O.P. (Violation of Probation).

I was finally ready to SURRENDER.
I was finally ready to TRUST.
And God knew it.

He knew what was in my heart.

I had finally reached the place of being tired. Truly tired. I was tired of running and only finding temporary relief from the tormenting pain.

Everything I had reached for had been so empty... but the void that I had so desperately been searching to fill was about to be filled... by a HEAVENLY FATHER, who was willing to meet me where I was. He extended His mercy, His grace, and His love to me.

Following my court hearing, I was sent to a rehabilitation center. Upon entering, I had already made up my mind to DO SOMETHING DIFFERENT. I knew there had to be CHANGE.

I took advantage of everything they had. Every resource and every option. I wanted them. I needed them. The desire for change had finally become stronger than the hold of addiction.

Even though during an earlier arrest I had sat with a chaplain and asked Jesus to come into my heart, I wasn't at the place of total surrender. I had gone through the verbal motions, but my heart was still heavily guarded. This time, through my surrender, healing and restoration began and trust was birthed.

Two years later, I entered into a relationship with a man who I felt was a gift from God. We lived together and had a beautiful little girl.

Along this new journey came a gift. Conviction. Conviction is a beautiful gift from the Holy Spirit. It spoke to me, and this time I wanted to listen. I was on the pursuit to truly know God, and to obey Him.

I was on a new journey. A journey of Change. A journey of true FREEDOM. A journey where I wanted to know more about this God who had reached through the darkness and brought me into the light. A God who loved me in my ashes and saw the beauty.

How could I not obey Him. He was the reason I was alive. So, to honor Him, my husband and I were married. And together we began to cultivate our relationship with God and then with each other. Aligning our life with the will of God allowed for healing and restoration to continue. Now, I have a relationship with my son, my younger siblings, and my mom.

Through the cleansing of my sins, by the precious BLOOD OF JESUS, I received pardon.
I received peace. I received strength.
And I received LIFE.

Areas which had once been dead, are now ALIVE!
They are alive because of His living water that runs
through them. Now every day is a new opportunity!

There are people who come into the place where I
work and tell me there's something about me that's
different. The atmosphere around me is different.
There's a light so bright, it illuminates the
atmosphere around me.

I know that it's Christ.
I choose to surround myself with worship, even at
work. Why would I not offer my worship to The
God who brought me out of death and into life?

He is so incredibly worthy!

I've had people who are tired of letting the
darkness overpower them kneel and ask how they
too, can know Jesus. Now, I've found purpose.

I used to ask God, "Why me God? Why did I have to
go through that?" He answered, "I called you out,
and through your pain you will help others."

I can't help but talk about Jesus.
God provided a way for me, and Jesus was that
way.

I've learned that Jesus doesn't become a part of "our life"... We become a part of HIS.

Now, I understand the redeeming words of the psalmist ...

"Though my father and mother abandoned me,
The Lord gathers me up."
Psalm 27:10

He Himself
is the atoning
sacrifice
for our sin

1 John 2:2

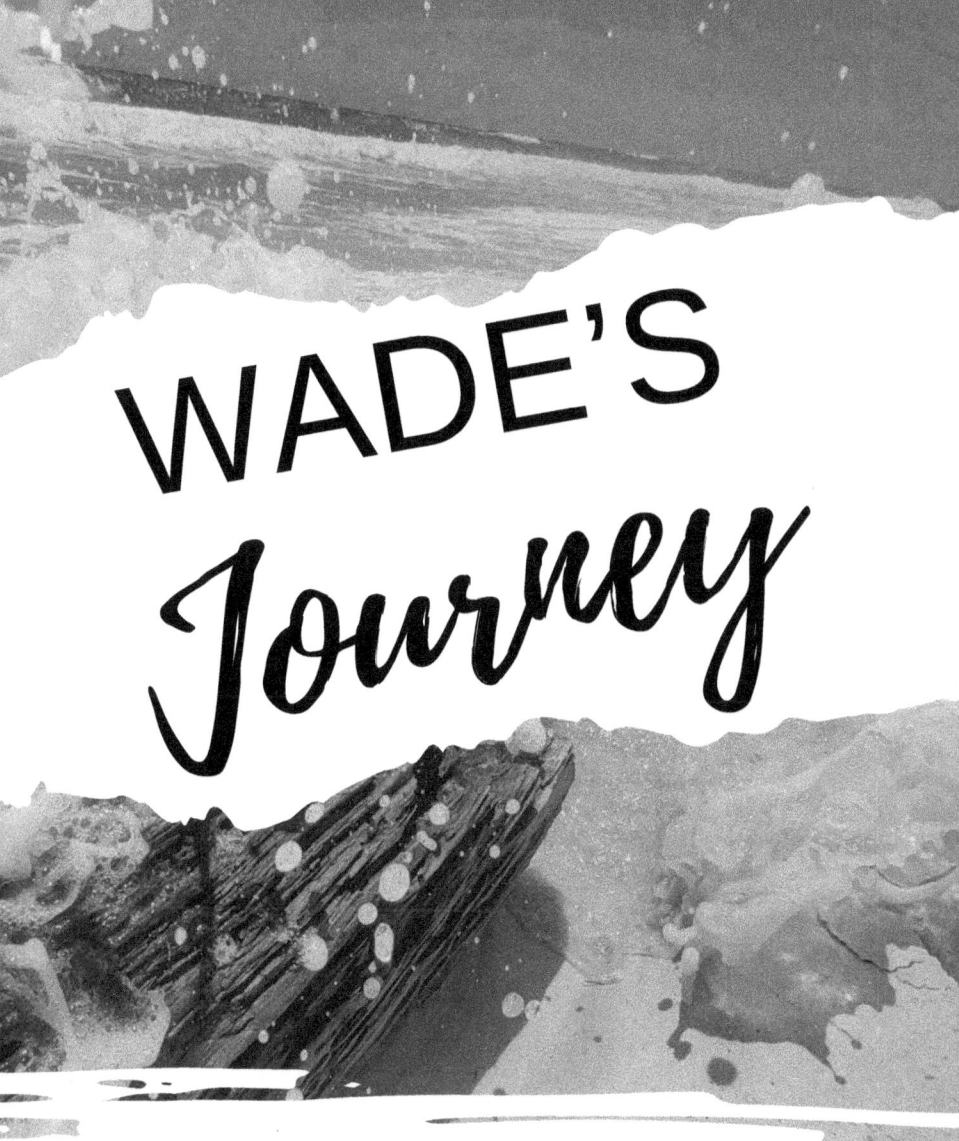

WADE'S

Journey

"Growing up wasn't easy,
but JOY held it together."

My dad and his siblings grew up with a father who was a violent alcoholic. Since drinking was a strong hold that he never sought to be freed from it later took his life in a horrible drunk driving accident.

Even though there had been years of abuse, I remember my grandmother being the one that held it all together. She was strong and I called her a saint. She had this thing of making sure there was always laughter in her home.

Not only did she raise my dad and his siblings, but she also cared for two of her own siblings who both had physical disabilities. Looking back, I understand it was her JOY that gave her strength. It was the glue that held our family together.

As a child, I remember my grandmother holding up two fingers; I saw it as the peace sign, and I used to tease her about it. She would say, "Wade, it's not a peace sign, It's a V. It stands for VICTORY... Victory in Jesus."

No matter where I was in our home, I could quietly say, "Victory in the name of..." and my grandmother, despite her location, would reply, "In the name of Jesus!"

Though to me, as a child, it was a game that I played with my grandmother. It planted seeds... powerful seeds. It taught me that victory can be found in Jesus.

Did I stay in that victory? No. I wandered. For several years I battled with my own addictions. Struggling and making so many wrong choices. I planted seeds during that time... seeds that led to nowhere. Seeds that were sown in dry places. My experiences were lifeless and yielded nothing but weeds.

At one point, during a time of relapse I had overdosed. The doctors told me that my kidneys had almost failed me. I was warned that if I was to continue, I would most surely die.

When I realized I couldn't do it alone; that I needed a strength beyond my own... I gave my life to Christ.

After I asked Him to cleanse me and become my Savior, I began to understand those almost forgotten words from my grandmother... "Victory in the name of Jesus."

In the middle of the storms while wrestling with the stumbling blocks of unhealthy thoughts, emotions, and seasons of discouragement, I've learned that victory CAN be found in Jesus.

I finally got it.

VICTORY IN JESUS is a discernment. One which my grandmother understood and did her best to instill in me as a child. I'm incredibly grateful.

Now, even when my journey sometimes hits a storm, my boat doesn't capsize because I've found true FREEDOM.

I'm allowing Jesus to guide the boat and control the rudder. I've learned that my mouth and my tongue are "the rudder". The steering force behind my responses. If not given much thought or consideration, they can become wild or even hurtful. They will speak either life or death.

Through my relationship with Christ, and reading the Bible, I've learned the importance of taming my tongue. I've realized the importance of taking unhealthy thoughts captive before they're allowed to wreak havoc.

Now, I desire to give Jesus my "Yes."

If I hear Him say, "Wade, I need you to do this...,"
I want to obey Him. I want to recognize the Holy
Spirit's voice and say "Yes" to whatever He is asking
of me. After all... He's the one that led me to my
Victory.

My prayer is that everyone will get a chance to live
life with Christ.

Don't try to do it alone...

There really is VICTORY IN JESUS!

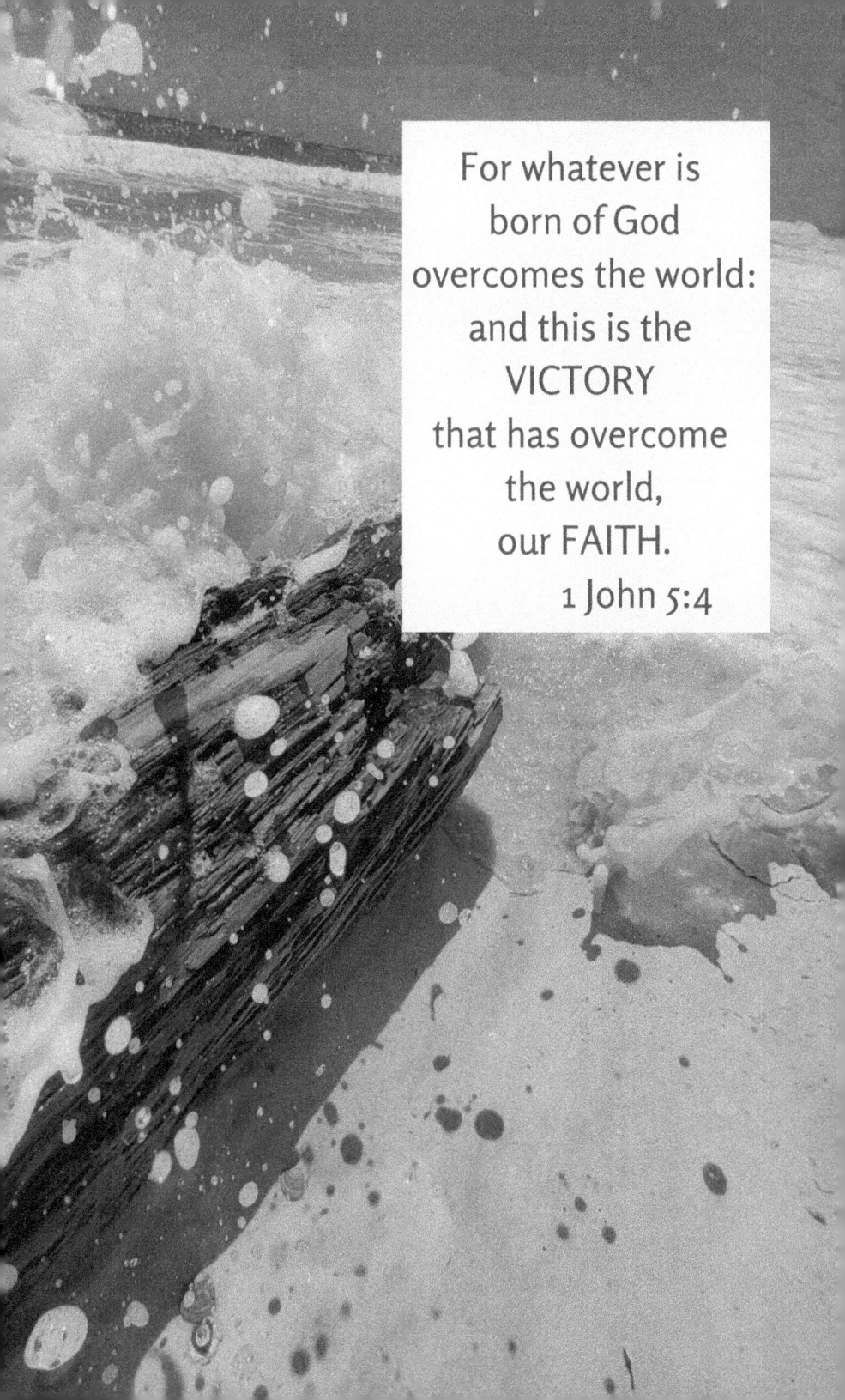

For whatever is
born of God
overcomes the world:
and this is the
VICTORY
that has overcome
the world,
our FAITH.
1 John 5:4

BRIAN'S *Journey*

"We found rest in the assurance
that we would one day
see our son."

In 2018, my girlfriend, now wife, and I were about to celebrate one of the most beautiful and memorable moments of our life; the birth of our son.

It hadn't been an easy pregnancy. Rebekah had been diagnosed with Factor 5 Liden which causes blood clotting. Due to being a high-risk pregnancy, she was receiving injections of blood thinners which seemed to be doing their job.

However, on February 21, 2019, we experienced a heartache that no parent should have to face. It was the hardest day of our lives.

My wife went into early labor by about eight weeks. After arriving at the hospital, the medical staff were unable to find a heartbeat. The next few hours that passed were the most difficult I had ever faced. It was tough watching Rebekah in so much pain, but it didn't end there. Within a few hours our son, Tucker Matthew Tracey, entered the world... stillborn.

Rebekah began to hemorrhage and fade in and out. She was given twenty-three pints of blood and plasma. I honestly thought I was going to lose her too.

I felt lost. Helpless. And scared.

I had no idea what the next step would be, but I found the courage to pray.

Rebekah's body did recover, and she finally became strong enough to be released from the hospital. But arriving home, our home that we had prepared for our son, felt empty.

That night as we arrived home without our son, I was so incredibly lost. Rebekah and I decided to go to Sunday night church. Honestly, it was because I just didn't know what else to do.

We had been attending church semi-regularly, but in this moment, I knew it was the place I needed to be. Looking back I understand it was God drawing us.

That night the sermon was about grief. As I listened, I began to understand that I needed to pursue God... as hard as I could. I knew in my heart that He would be the only one able to help us through such horrible heartache and pain.

After service, the pain didn't immediately stop. And in the days to come, Rebekah and I played the blame game within ourselves and toward each other. We had questions, so many unanswered questions. We were riding on a roller coaster of emotions. We were unstable, and so was our relationship.

Even still, God kept nudging.

Romans 14:19 teaches:

"Therefore, let us keep on pursuing those things that bring peace and that lead to building up one another."

He kept pulling us; toward Himself, to be an active part of the body of Christ, to grow in His Word, and to find rest in the assurance that we would one day see our son. We found peace in knowing that one day, we would all spend eternity TOGETHER.

We grew, and wanted to do what was right by God, and to obey and honor His design of marriage. Rebekah and I married. We knew we were taking our commitment from a lifetime to an eternity together.

One month later we were pregnant again. Honestly, at first, I was scared and anxious. I was nervous yet excited all at the same time.

We both decided it would be best for Rebekah if she stopped working. With her being on bedrest, we were determined to find a way to make it work. In our heart we knew that God was giving us a gift. We trusted Him. We knew that He would make a way and provide for us during this time,

And He did.

On February 27th, 2022, Rebekah was scheduled to be induced. The night before, I had found a quiet place where I got down on my knees and I prayed aloud this prayer:

"God, I pray with everything I have. Please bring this baby into the world, safe and healthy. Please keep my wife safe and healthy. You have got us this far. Please, I ask You with everything I have. Amen."

The next morning we arrived at the hospital. As we were getting checked in and Rebekah was being prepped for the induction, we heard these words from the staff, "Well, it seems like the baby wants to come out on her own. You're already dilated to four centimeters."

After an all-day labor, around seven in the evening, our baby girl was coming! There was still one more obstacle standing in the way. Our baby was stuck in the birth canal with her hand wrapped over her face and the umbilical cord tucked in her hand.

Our daughter's heart rate began to drop. The midwife and nursing staff were around my wife, trying to help get our baby girl out. A few moments later I heard a nurse yell, "We need to get the doctor in here, she's not coming out!"

It was at that moment, as fear gripped my mind, and emotions began to flood my heart, that I knew who I needed to reach out towards.

I quickly made my way over to the bathroom door and screamed a prayer to God...
"Please God! We need You! Right here! Right now! This is what we've been praying for! We need You NOW!"

Within seconds the midwife yelled, "Dad, get over here, she's coming out!" Minutes later, we welcomed our Ella Ruth.

She was alive... and she was healthy. This was an answer from God.

Through this unimaginable season, one of the toughest I have ever faced, God helped me get through it. He gave me strength that I needed. He gave me faith stronger than my fears.

A faith that was greater than depression. A faith greater than anxiety,

Today our baby girl is fourteen months old. Our path to being great parents is being laid one step at a time, by God, as He teaches us daily.

The same God that we learned can be trusted through the pain, through the confusion, and through the heartache. He offered us peace.

When there seems to be no answers...
God IS the answer.

The light shines in the darkness,
and the darkness has not overcome it.
John 1:5

Harley's *Journey*

"But today, I am a
SURVIVOR!"

I used to be the "strong" one.

The one that moved abused women and children into my home to help them get away. To help them find safety. I used to help them pass their social-work visits. I was foster approved, all while working at a local department store.

I worked hard.

I was independent.

I remember weeping, as the women that I had helped, returned to their abusers. I didn't understand. Why? Why would they go back? Why were they putting themselves and their children through it again? Why would they return after being completely out, away from their abuser? Why did all of them return to something they had begged for help to get out of?

I never understood.

It's hard to understand something when you've never experienced it. Even then your understanding is limited, because everyone's story is different.

Let me rewind for a moment.

At the age of seventeen I moved out on my own. I thought I was independent. I thought I was happy. In hindsight I realize now that I had no goals. No direction. Just living life, working to provide for myself and hanging out with friends who I felt were "sisters" to me.

One in particular was Mariah. We were roommates. We were ALWAYS there for each other. It was Mariah and I against the world!

In my life I had known *of* God, but I didn't personally know God. I was straying... far away. Even though I thought I had everything I needed, I was wrong.

I'll never forget the date. It was the twenty-fifth of November 2010, Thanksgiving Day. In one single, completely unexpected phone call... life as I knew it came crashing down.

My friend. My closest friend. My sister. Mariah... was gone.

I didn't even get to tell her goodbye.

Only one month and one week, before that phone call, Mariah and I had been arguing. Arguing over who she was dating. She had decided to move out.

When I received the call, I was at my Nana's. I remember crawling into her bed, weeping and laying in the fetal position, crying, "Mariah. Mariah is dead."

Another "sister" was Aimee. After hearing the news of Mariah's death, Aimee loaded up her family and drove to my Nana's. She didn't leave my side.

Mariah's' death was the beginning of my downward spiral.

In an attempt to numb the pain, hurt, and confusion... I drank. From the time I woke up until the time I laid down for bed, I drank. The drinking finally slowed down, but in an attempt to stay away from alcohol I tried to keep myself busy. If I wasn't busy, I cried. Over and over, I cried.

I became so tired of crying. I went in search for happiness. I wanted it so badly. I attempted to find it wherever I could. Unfortunately, within a few months, it led me to *him*.

Have you ever heard the saying "The devil comes like a thief in the night?" Boy, did he!

It began one night, during one of my attempts to stay busy. I was painting the inside of my house and felt the urge to smoke, but had ran out of cigarettes. I made a drive to the nearby gas station.

Who knew that with ONE CHOICE my life would change forever.

I spent the next hour talking to an old acquaintance and their friend; a guy. Prior to Mariah's death I would have never looked twice, but at this point in time, it felt right.

Even though something was telling me to stay away, I chose not to listen. Looking back, I recognize it was the voice of the Holy Spirit trying desperately to guide me.

I thought I was in love. Before long, he had moved in with me. After only three months, we set a wedding date. I had been completely swept away. Charmed.

When the abuse began, he tried to convince me that I was crazy. I wasn't allowed to have friends over for visits. If I questioned him, he became angry. The only thing I was allowed to do without him was work. It wasn't long until I wasn't allowed to do that either; he talked me into quitting my job.

He often went through my phone, checking all of my calls, text messages, and social media. Nothing was private. He instructed me to delete any and all pictures that contained men. He forced me to delete any guy friends from social media.

My girl friends were even made off limits eventually. Aimee was the only friend that I was able to talk to and she was quick to share her concerns with me, especially prior to our wedding.

Aimee asked me, "Do you really want to get married?" I told her that I felt like it was too late. Too late for me to change my mind. I felt stuck. Everything had already been paid for. She begged me not to go through with it, but I did... in spite of the unsettling feelings that lay in my gut.

On the day of the wedding I remember my dad saying, "Just say the word and we will leave. The car is fueled up and your Momma can tell everyone after we're gone."

Again, God was offering a way out, but I responded with...
"I'm okay. I can't disappoint everyone."

We were married.

The very next day, even though so much about him had already changed, more was yet to come. It was even more horrible.

I was his property.

Around people I was his idol, but in their absence, I was his trash. I absolutely hated when people would leave because their presence made me feel safe.

People would say things to me like, "You're so lucky! I wish I had your life!" Be careful comparing your life to someone else's. Appearances can be deceiving.

In the months that followed, he cheated. He had relationships with numerous women, even going so far as to include his own family.

When I approached him, he would say, "You're too fat" and "I'm not attracted to you."

Shortly after, I moved in with my stepsister, but it was only the beginning of our many breakups that followed.

Remember the women I spoke of at the beginning of my story? I was now one of them.

I struggled to find a normal life.

The longer we were apart, the healthier I became.

However, out of the fear of becoming a "statistic", I continued to fall for his deceit over and over again. The verbal and emotional abuse continued.

Before long, I was pregnant. I was happy yet scared at the same time. I had hopes that maybe my pregnancy would change everything. Maybe this baby would bring about the normality I was longing for.

However, I was blinded by my hopes, and his deceit. One horrific night while I was pregnant, he allowed a pit bull that he had been raising to fight, to attack me. I remember laying in the fetal position covered by a thin blanket, attempting to protect my unborn child. All while he stood in a doorway... laughing.

After what felt like hours, he finally called his dog off me, took the dog, and left. I rose, bloody and hysterical. Neighbors witnessed the aftermath of the bloody attack as I made my way to my car. My Nana witnessed the aftermath.

Yet still, he had a hold on me.

I understand now that it's the fear and manipulation that keeps you frozen. I was made to feel unwanted by anyone. Unworthy of love. Worthless.

The days, weeks, and months that followed were filled with his deceit and manipulation.

I was broken, scared, and felt very much alone.

Just prior to my daughter's birth I hit a tipping point after finding him in our home with several girls. I finally broke. In my brokenness came the strength to leave. My parents helped me escape and within a week I filed for divorce.

For approximately two to three months I was strong. My baby was born, and life finally felt normal. Peace had finally arrived. However, his new avenue of manipulation, his hold, now included our child. He would say, "Let me help you with the baby."

I wanted to believe the best. However, it was his trickery. His new way of sliding back into my life.

My husband's abuse did not stop with me. He assaulted women. He assaulted teens. A few years later, after he was registered as a sex offender, there were still those who thought I was the crazy one. They didn't think he would stoop so low, but I knew the truth.

The thing about abusers is that they are really good at wearing a mask. They're professionals at putting on a facade when other people are around. Their personalities can change faster than a light switch. They are masters of deceit. As his cheating and sexual assaults worsened, so did his violence.

As for me, depression worsened, loneliness deepened, and self-worth vanished.

I lied to everyone while appearing to be okay, because he told me that he would kill me if I ever took our children and left. Even his own mother told me, "I feel so bad for you and your girls. He will kill you before you ever get out."
I believed her.

I lost all hope and faith. I lost myself. I was tired. Tired of being hurt, tired of his anger, tired of losing things he would shatter and break during his rage, and tired of his manipulation.
It's a stronghold.

A stronghold that's from the pits of hell itself. It ensnares your mind and heart. It strips away your strength, hope, aspirations, and faith. It distances you from your family and friends. It isolates you while slowly stripping away your inner being.

After eight years. Eight long years... I began to question God.

If God was real, why would this be happening? Why were my girls and I having to go through this?

I began to tell myself that this was my punishment. Punishment for things I had done when I was younger. As unhealthy as it was, that kind of thinking became my reasoning for the pain.

I began writing letters to my girls. I truly believed he would kill me. I believed that by leaving letters for my girls that one day, when they were older, they would have something to remind them of how much I loved them.

Even though I was alive physically, I had already died emotionally. He had broken me.

However, on a cold morning in January, while I was attempting to get our girls ready for school, he entered into another one of his rages. This time, in the heat of his rage he actually hurt himself. As he stood there, bleeding and yelling in front of our children, there was a sudden strength that rose up within me.

A strength I had never felt before.

I knew I had to do something. I knew my children could no longer live in such an abusive, manipulative, and frightening environment.

Even though I thought God had abandoned me, He had not!

He had protected me. He had protected my children.

Today, I AM A SURVIVOR!

That cold morning in January, after receiving the supernatural strength to finally leave him, I was led in the direction of true FREEDOM!

The path wasn't without obstacles. Growth is never a smooth transition, but God was with me every step of the way.

What's so beautiful about having a relationship with God is that He doesn't require us to come to him "baggage free, or all cleaned up." Instead, He provides a way for that, through His Son, Jesus.

Even though I felt insignificant, unworthy, unloved, and unwanted, God didn't see me that way. He offered me His redemption, healing, restoration, and love, free from manipulation and fear.

When I finally reached the place of willingness to step into the life God had for me, all of my broken pieces began to heal. Strongholds began to break, and true strength, hope, and faith began to grow.

That cold morning in January, through the supernatural strength that rose up within me, I was finally willing to step out of the darkness, out of the embarrassment, the shame, and the guilt... to make a step towards God, and He met me there.

He calls me HIS DAUGHTER!

He equips me with strength.

He clothes me in His righteousness.

Through my relationship with my Heavenly Father, I have learned that unforgiveness keeps me under someone else's power. Even though I have struggled with forgiveness, God through His mercy and grace is teaching me how to let go, and how to forgive.

I have learned how to set personal boundaries to ensure that it never happens again.

I've grown.

Now, my life is one that I never thought I could have, or deserved. I'm remarried. My husband loves the Lord, and together, we've made God the foundation of our home.

Every day my girls live in a home that is safe. They see their mommy healthy, both emotionally and physically. They're experiencing a home that's filled with unconditional love.

We pray together as a family.

We grow in our relationship with God as a family.

Even though their biological father still attempts to make threats, I know we're protected by God and that we have nothing to fear.

I am no longer alone...

"The Lord is the one who is shepherding me;
I lack nothing. He causes me to lie down
in pastures of green grass; He guides me
beside quiet waters. He revives my life;
He leads me in the pathways that are righteous
for the sake of His name. Even when I walk
through the valley of deep darkness,
I will not be afraid because You are with me.
Your rod and Your staff, they comfort me.
You prepare a table before me, even in the
presence of my enemies. You anoint my head
with oil; my cup overflows. Truly, goodness and
gracious love will pursue me
all the days of my life,
and I will remain in the Lord's house forever!"
Psalms 23 (ISV)

Amen.

That we may no longer be children, tossed back and forth, carried about with every wind of doctrine, by the trickery of men, in the cunning, craftiness of deceitful plotting,

but, speaking the truth in love, may grow up in all things into Him who is the head - Christ
Ephesians 4:14, 15

Stan's

Journey

"Addiction is real."

I was raised by parents who worked hard and instilled a good work ethic in me. We had a good family unit. As a child my mom, grandmother, and aunt took me to church every time the doors were open.

For over ten years I was sent to a private Christian school where I studied the Bible and memorized a scripture each week. Early on, I knew about God.

My dad, grandpa, and uncle all worked hard. But every day after work they would come home, go into their garages or shops, and drink beer. Most days they drank until bedtime. On weekends, they would hit the bars. The result would be fighting and arguing between the women and men of the family.

One time after a fight I asked my dad if he was an alcoholic, because my mom had called him one. He replied "No, I'm not." He continued to tell me that he gave half of his money to my mom so that she could pay the bills. He told me that alcoholics were bums living under the overpass and in railroad yards, drinking day and night. He told me that he had earned the right to drink his beer and smoke his pot because that's what working men do. He even added that his job was hot, and he needed the hydration.

So... I admired him. Along with my grandpa and uncle.

I wanted to be like them. Still, I was in church all the time.

At the age of thirteen I began working my first paid job. I was washing dishes at the local restaurant. Soon after, my dad started giving me beer and pot. He said he was proud of his hardworking son.

I was growing up seeing both sides, but was too young to truly understand.

At the age of eighteen I began traveling the country as a welder doing government and union jobs. When I left my hometown I left not only my family, but also my church and God.

From the age of eighteen to twenty-eight I made money. A lot of money. And I spent a lot as well. For me it was about sex, drugs, and rock & roll. For a while it seemed good... even fun.

Later I returned to my hometown. It wasn't long before I met a girl that had two baby boys. We decided to marry and settle down. For a while I was able to cut down on the drinking, but I continued to smoke pot daily and occasionally did a little cocaine.

The girl I had met struggled with being faithful, but even though she was having affairs I loved our kids. I was willing to make it work. Before long, the pain and disappointments led me back to drinking. After fourteen years of marriage, on our anniversary, she packed her bags and moved in with another man, leaving the children with me.

Drinking and increasing my drug use followed. They became my excuse for not knowing how to deal with the hurt of abandonment. In an attempt to hide my substance abuse from my boys, after work each day I would stop at a local hotel lounge near our apartment.

The hotel manager befriended me. She and I spent time getting drunk and high, and soon we moved in together. The night club scene became a common pastime and so did the lifestyle attached to it. Yet, we were able to live large on the money we were making.

We were married at the Opryland Hotel in Nashville on a beautiful balcony. Condos, hot tubs, parties, and new vehicles became the norm. We worked hard and partied hard. I felt like I was on top of the world.
But living large is expensive. Addiction is expensive. Both lead you down a deep dark path that ends up nowhere... Quicker than you can imagine.

The owner of the company I was working for retired, and the company closed. I was out of a job. Shortly after, both my grandmother and dad passed away. And just like that, my life began spinning out of control.

I knew I had to do something, but on my own I wasn't strong enough. I talked to my wife about entering rehab. Instead she persuaded me to take a "little green pill"... Oxycontin. I had never heard of it before, but I quickly came to know it all too well. Addicted from the start, I jumped out of the frying pan and straight into the fire. It was Hell.

We lost the condo, and as the addiction grew, my ability to function decreased.

To keep from becoming homeless, we moved into my parent's old house where I had grown up.

Before long, our area was preparing for Hurricane Ivan. Suddenly my world was changing again. While others were preparing for the storm by stockpiling food and water, we were making sure we had a two-week supply of oxies, Lortabs, heroin, or any other kind of opiates we could find. Without it we thought we would die.

Addiction is REAL.

And it will quickly control you, while also sucking life right out of you.

After the hurricane there was so much work in the area; cutting trees, repairing roofs, gathering debris. I started my own business repairing and rebuilding screen rooms and pool enclosures. Even though I was making a thousand dollars a day, I was spending a thousand dollars a day... just to keep us from getting dope sick.

"Dope sick."

Yeah, it's real. That's when your body is so used to the drug that if you slow down, withdrawals begin. Everything hurts. Everything. Your hair, your nails, cramps, sweats, diarrhea, and convulsions. It's intense, and staying in bed seems like the only option. I would go to sleep at night with the next morning's dose of drugs on the nightstand already prepared. All I had to do was wake up, roll over, and dose. Ten minutes later I would be okay enough to make coffee and get ready for work. My wife's morning routine was the same.

Hurricane work doesn't last forever. As the work dried up and the economy struggled, we started selling everything we had. Appliances in our home, right down to the electrical wiring. We traded vehicles for drugs. Then we started stealing, scamming, begging, scrapping, and even prostituting.

There wasn't anything we wouldn't do, short of killing, to get the next fix.

I honestly don't remember 2006 through 2007.

In March of 2008, after doping all night on a Friday, I woke up on Saturday morning needing a fix. I decided to try walking to a nearby store to beg, and I ended up committing a crime. I knew I was in deep... Deeper than I had ever been.

In that moment I cried out to God.

I knew in my heart that I hadn't been raised to be like this and that God hadn't created me to live like this. Something in me knew that if there wasn't a quick change, my end would be bad. Real bad.

I was sick. I was tired.

I was sick and tired of being sick and tired.

I was terrified!

In that moment I said, "God, if you save me, I will spend the rest of my life seeking you and serving you."

I went to a nearby church, talked with the pastor there, and accepted Christ.

However, I was still making my own choices instead of doing what God would want.

I did start attending church and reading the Bible. My wife, however, wanted nothing to do with the church and soon left. All the while, I kept using drugs to deal with the withdrawals.

I prayed. I asked God for help. I asked for a way out.

On July 13th, 2010, I had my last drink. Yet it wasn't until 2011 that I was able to put down the other drugs. I was a "dry drunk" as some call it. On my own I struggled. A program known as Celebrate Recovery came to my church. I jumped in. It was through that program that I gained the strength to truly break FREE.

Everything began to make sense. I began learning about the roots attached to the underlying reasons why I had started using drugs in the first place and why it had taken me so long to break free from them.

Today I can truly say, "I am free."

Jesus referred to Himself in Luke 4:18, 19 as this...

"The Spirit of the Lord is upon Me because He has anointed Me to preach the gospel to the poor, He has sent Me to heal the brokenhearted, to proclaim liberty to the captives and recovery of sight to the blind, to set at liberty those who are oppressed, to proclaim the acceptable year of the Lord."

That's who Jesus is!

That's why He came... so that in our weakness, selfishness, pride, and addictions, through Him... we can be MADE FREE.

I also learned that Jesus is the WAY, the TRUTH, and the LIFE. No one comes to the Father, except through Him. (John 14:6)

After accepting Jesus as my Savior, growing in His Word, and in my personal relationship with Him, I was able to break free... Free from what once had me bound.

I am remarried. I have a beautiful and loving wife, four children, and a home near the water. I also have a job in ministry. My dream job! We feed the homeless, counsel addicts, and share the LOVE OF GOD with them.

God is restoring all of what the enemy had stolen: my life, my dignity, my reputation, my health, and my self-respect.

Today, nothing, absolutely nothing, is more important than my sobriety and my very intimate and personal relationship with Jesus.

I will serve Him, for the rest of my life!

I have set before you
life and death
blessing and cursing
choose life
so that you and your
descendants
may live...
Deuteronomy 30:19

Jay's Journey

"Suicide lost. Love won."

"My daughter doesn't play with white trash."

I remember those words very clearly.

It was a summer day and I had just moved into the neighborhood. Until this point in my life I was being raised by my grandparents who were raising me in church. The fear of God was being ingrained in me.

However, their home didn't always feel safe. I remember around age five being taught that if my Dad came for a visit I was to hide. I knew that hiding place well. It was in the back of my grandmother's closet. It was dark and just before the door would close; my grandmother would remind me to be quiet, very quiet.

I remember light would seep through the cracks in the door, allowing me to see my grandmother's shoes. The light kept me from being in complete darkness, and somehow being able to see her shoes provided comfort.

At the age of eight, I suddenly found myself living with my mom and stepdad. I honestly don't even remember the transition.

There was a visit; and then what seemed to be the very next day, I was riding a bus from a new school to a new home... my mom's home.

On the bus I saw a girl who lived down the street and I couldn't wait to walk down and ask if she could play. I was excited! For me, it was a new adventure!

At the age of eight I stood there, only knocking twice, waiting for my new friend to answer the door. Instead, the person who stood before me was a tall woman, with dark flowing hair. With excitement I asked my question before even giving her time to say hello, but she responded quickly with these words, "My daughter doesn't play with white trash," then she closed the door.

I stood there for a moment, processing what had just happened. I honestly wasn't sure what she meant, but I did know what "trash" was. As I turned to walk away, I questioned. "Had I just been compared to trash? Why?"

Unfortunately, it didn't take long for that revelation. I quickly learned that police visits to our home were sometimes common. Domestic Violence.

There's a name for it now, but in those days, it was just another visit to break up another fight. Sometimes, my stepdad was encouraged to take a drive to allow time for he, or my Mom, to cool off. However, most times it was just a request to "settle down" because the neighbors were being disturbed.

The neighbors. But what about the children inside of that home? How were they being affected?

At the age of fourteen, at the beginning of my freshman year of high school, and after so many moves, and innumerable fights, satan wedged his way further into my life. A local neighborhood drug dealer introduced me to pills: Yellow Jackets, Black Mollys, and then to Marijuana. He told me that he would supply me with anything I wanted, as long as I sold for him on my school campus.

So, I did.

I didn't consider the consequences. I didn't consider the danger I would be putting others in. I only thought of myself. Only one thing, that when I "used", I didn't have to think about the chaos around me.

I would arrive home from school, go to my room, separate the seeds from the weed, then sit, listen to music, and draw. It became my peace. At least, that's what I thought.

However, "peace" was actually getting even further out of my reach.

There were days where I couldn't even remember what I had done. My grades were failing, and I felt sick almost every day. I struggled with memory issues, and had come to a place where I didn't care what happened to me.

Finally, a year later, I was arrested. In my possession were a few pills, a bag of weed, and a few one-dollar bills in a bag. They arrested me for possession with intent to sell. There in my school's office I was handcuffed, then placed in the back of a police car.

When I arrived at "Juvie Hall", that's what it was known as, I could only think of one thing, "My family will be disappointed in me." It felt like hours before I saw a family member. I honestly don't know the conversations my parents had with police, but after a few hours I was released.

The end result was three years of probation with community service. The judge sternly told me that if he saw my face again, it would mean jail time. Even though I had dodged physical jail, I had crawled deeper into my emotional jail. I had created distrust between myself and my parents, and to me, that was all that I had.

I had sunk deeper into depression.

On December 20th of 1983, five days before Christmas, I wrote a poem entitled, Masquerade. Here's a piece of that writing,

"This world is like a masquerade with silly mask and love that tends to fade. No, you won't find forgiveness here. No one will forget what you have done, and to the innocent, they try to take away their values and push to make them run. Though the clocks keep on ticking, my whole life has stopped. I have no desire or will to continue with this game, so I handed in the pieces and turned in my name."

As I battled with depression, I also battled suicidal thoughts. Looking back, I'm so extremely grateful that the seeds of Truth had been planted within me by my Grandparents. I feared God. I feared going to hell. So, instead I wrote about it. Writing became my outlet, instead of the drugs.

A few weeks later, on a Wednesday, my stepmother showed up at our house. I remember being out in a field mowing the grass. It was in the middle of summer, and very hot. As I watched her get out of the car, and began walking the sidewalk to our house I wondered why she was there.

She had arrived alone. My Dad wasn't with her. I knew her, but not very well. I admired her though. She was peaceful. When my siblings and I would visit with our Dad, she would take us to church.

Remember the beginning of my story I shared a bit about hiding from my Dad in my grandmother's closet. Years later, my Dad had married my stepmom, and she was a Christian. She loved the Lord, and through her walk with God, my Dad later accepted Christ as His Savior too.

On this day, a few moments after talking with my Mom, my stepmom walked over to me and asked if I would like to come to a "Youth Meeting". I had no idea what a youth meeting was, but I responded, "Sure."

That night, my life was changed forever.
It was Movie Night, and the other teens were all gathered together in a large room of the church. There was free popcorn and drinks. I remember the adult leaders being very welcoming, and the other teens being friendly.

The movie shown was, The Thief In The Night. By the end of that movie I knew I wanted change. Talk about being "Scared Straight"... I was scared straight! And even though I had responded to the altar call, it was due to my emotions, without a clear understanding of why.

However, it was only the beginning of what was about to happen.

After the youth meeting, on the way home, my stepmother asked if I would like to attend church with them on Sunday. I immediately said, "Yes."

I knew something was different. I was feeling something besides pain, and I wanted more.
As an adult I now understand it was Psalm 34:8 in action... "Oh, taste and see that the Lord is Good!"

I had tasted.
It was a taste of God and the peace that He offered, and I wanted more.

That Sunday, the church was incredibly packed. There was a well-known evangelist visiting. Actually, he was there for a weeklong Revival.

Church began. The choir sang. And as the atmosphere was slowly changing around me, I could feel it. It was remarkable to me.

Suddenly, right in the middle of his talking, the strangest thing happened. The evangelist turned, walked straight to me, (out of hundreds of people), stopped, and pointed at me. He then asked this question, "If you were to die right now, will you go to Heaven?"

Without hesitation my response was, "I don't know." He then said, "Then go to the altar." I went straight there... but I wasn't alone.

He met me there, along with a few other people. They prayed over me, as they led me in saying a prayer. I asked Jesus to forgive me of my sins. I asked Him to wash me clean, and to come into my heart and live there forever.

After saying that prayer, there are no words to completely describe what happened next. In an instant, I was face down in the carpet, tears pouring down my face, and an OVERWHELMING PEACE enveloped me. I felt a peace like never before. I wept. And wept. And wept.

Later, I remember laughter began to roll out of my mouth. At first, I didn't understand it, but it was something I had no control over. It was just a sweet and gentle laughter. It was a beautiful gift from the Holy Spirit.

It had been a long time since I had laughed. And in that moment, it was such a pure, and joyous laughter that came from the center of my inner most being.

When I finally came to my feet, three hours had passed. THREE HOURS. I couldn't believe it!

What I'm about to share is not at all to disrespect my parents. It is only to share my journey to Freedom... not only for myself, but also for my family.

When I walked out of the church my stepdad was there in the parking lot. As soon as I entered the car, he told me that my Mom was mad because I didn't come out of the church right away when it was over.

Neither of them had any idea that I had just spent the last three hours with my face in the carpet, being visited by the Holy Spirit... and at the age of fifteen, I didn't know how to respond, or explain it to him. The peace, the joy, the life that was now in me I never wanted to lose.

When we arrived home my Mom met me on the porch, and in her anger, I was slapped and fell back onto the ground. From that moment, I knew I had to do something different. I wanted to hold on to what I had experienced at church.

A few days later I ran away.

I had no plan, and no idea where I would go. I just wanted to be anywhere but there.

I found myself with a friend who encouraged me to talk with her grandmother. I didn't want to talk with an adult, I just wanted to hide out. I know now, it had to be the Holy Spirit that encouraged me to agree to talk with her. She was gentle, and she was wise. She was able to talk me into calling my Dad.

That was the beginning of my living with him and my stepmother. Church became a normal part of my life. At first, the shame of being on probation kept me in a bubble. However, that was short lived, because the people at this church LOVED on me. They didn't see me as anything but a girl who Christ loved... just like them.

I was taught how to work with the Puppet Ministry, and I loved it! I became a part of other ministries as well. I was loved. I was trusted. It was truly medicine for my soul.

During that summer I grew spiritually. I was learning so much from God's Word, and God's people.

When school started that August, I was different.

It wasn't at first; but eventually the school administration recognized the change. Teachers encouraged me to continue on the path that I was on. I found that peer pressure was never an issue because the LIFE that I now had, I was not letting go of.

I remember very late one night my Mom showed up at my Dad's. As she knocked on my window, it became apparent that she was very drunk. I questioned how she was even able to drive herself there. I asked her to leave. She wept. She asked me to come home.

Later, after she drove away, I layed there. I began praying for her. I asked the Lord to show her the same peace that He had shown to me. I asked Him not to let her die until she was able to know peace and was able to live in it.

I wanted so badly for her to feel what it was like to have a relationship with Christ. I wanted her to experience His peace, and to live years within that peace. So, I prayed. For several years I prayed. God hears our prayers. He cares about the desires of our heart. He's Faithful.

Here. In 2023, my grandparents are in Heaven. My Dad is in Heaven. My stepmother is in Heaven. My brother is in Heaven... and so many others. Guess where my mom is? Here, on earth... LIVING IN PEACE.

She loves the Lord! She accepted Him as her Father. She's learned so much about the Bible. She's active in her church family, and is involved in Women's Bible Studies.

I once heard a pastor ask this question...

"If you were to lose something valuable, would you take a quick look around and if you didn't find it, just walk off and say, 'oh, well'? No. Instead, you would continue to search for it. You would move things out of the way if that's what it took. You would not give up the search until you found it."

That's what my Mom did. She didn't give up the search, even when satan relentlessly tried to make her feel ashamed and full of guilt, she continued to search. She didn't give up! She didn't walk away. She pushed forward. She grew. She trusted. She healed. And now, she's RESTORED!

On January 25th, 1999, during a service; the minister was sharing out of Isaiah chapter 58. He was teaching about fasting, but when he stopped reading, something drew me to continue on. When I reached verses six through fourteen it was as though the words were being spoken straight to me... straight from God, and into the deepest part of my heart.

It spoke about the fast that is acceptable to God... and it lists the things God wants us to do. It then says this...

"THEN your light shall break forth like the morning. Your healing shall spring forth speedily,
And your righteousness shall go before you.
The glory of the Lord shall be your rear guard."

It gives more instructions of what God expects from us, then He promises this...

"Then your light shall dawn in the darkness,
and your darkness shall be as the noonday
(the BRIGHTEST PART)
And The Lord will guide you continually, and satisfy
your soul in dry places, and make strong your
bones; and you shall be like a watered garden, and
like a spring of water, whose waters do not fail.
[12] And those who shall be of you (your sons and
your daughters) shall build the old waste places;
you shall raise up the foundations of many
generations, and you shall be called THE REPAIRER
of the breach, THE RESTORER of paths to dwell in."

I remember crying so hard I felt as though I
couldn't breathe. I rose from my seat, and laid in
the floor with my face to the carpet. I told God that
I was receiving that as a direct promise from Him to
me. A direct promise to my children. A direct
promise to my extended family.

My Freedom Journey wasn't one just for me. It was
also for my family. Generational curses were to be
broken.

I had a job to do. God taught me how to grow, and
learn from His Word, and as I grew, He was
FAITHFUL!

He did exactly what He said to me that night through Isaiah 58... He REPAIRED and RESTORED!

My mom was healed. She was set FREE from abuse, from loneliness, from fear, from all of the generational baggage she had carried for so many years. That same baggage that had been allowed to bind to her children, and to her grandchildren.

God, through His promise and in His faithfulness, provided healing and restoration to our family. My daughters don't live in domestic violence, or with substance abuse. My grandchildren aren't being raised in domestic violence, or around substance abuse.

It's all because of one reason, the promise that can be found in Isaiah 58... if we allow the Lord to "guide us"... then He's faithful to do the rest.

One of the most powerful passages I have ever read is found in Isaiah 61;

> "...that there should be given to them
> that mourn in Zion,
> glory instead of ashes,
> the oil of JOY to the mourning,

the garment of praise for the spirit of heaviness;
and they shall be called generations of
righteousness,
the planting of the Lord for His glory!
And they shall build the old waste places,
they shall raise up those that were before made
desolate,
and they shall renew the desert cities,
even those that had been desolate for many
generations.

...

They shall inherit the land a second time,
and everlasting joy shall be upon their head!"

I'm believing that my "latter shall be greater than my beginning," Haggai 2:9.

God is the only one who can cause LIGHT to burst through darkness. I don't want my pain to mean nothing. I want God to use it to help others.

I ROSE FROM THE ASHES.
My Mom ROSE FROM THE ASHES!
And so can ANYONE ELSE!

Then your light
shall break fourth
as the morning,
and your healing
shall spring forth
speedily...
Isaiah 58:8 (a)

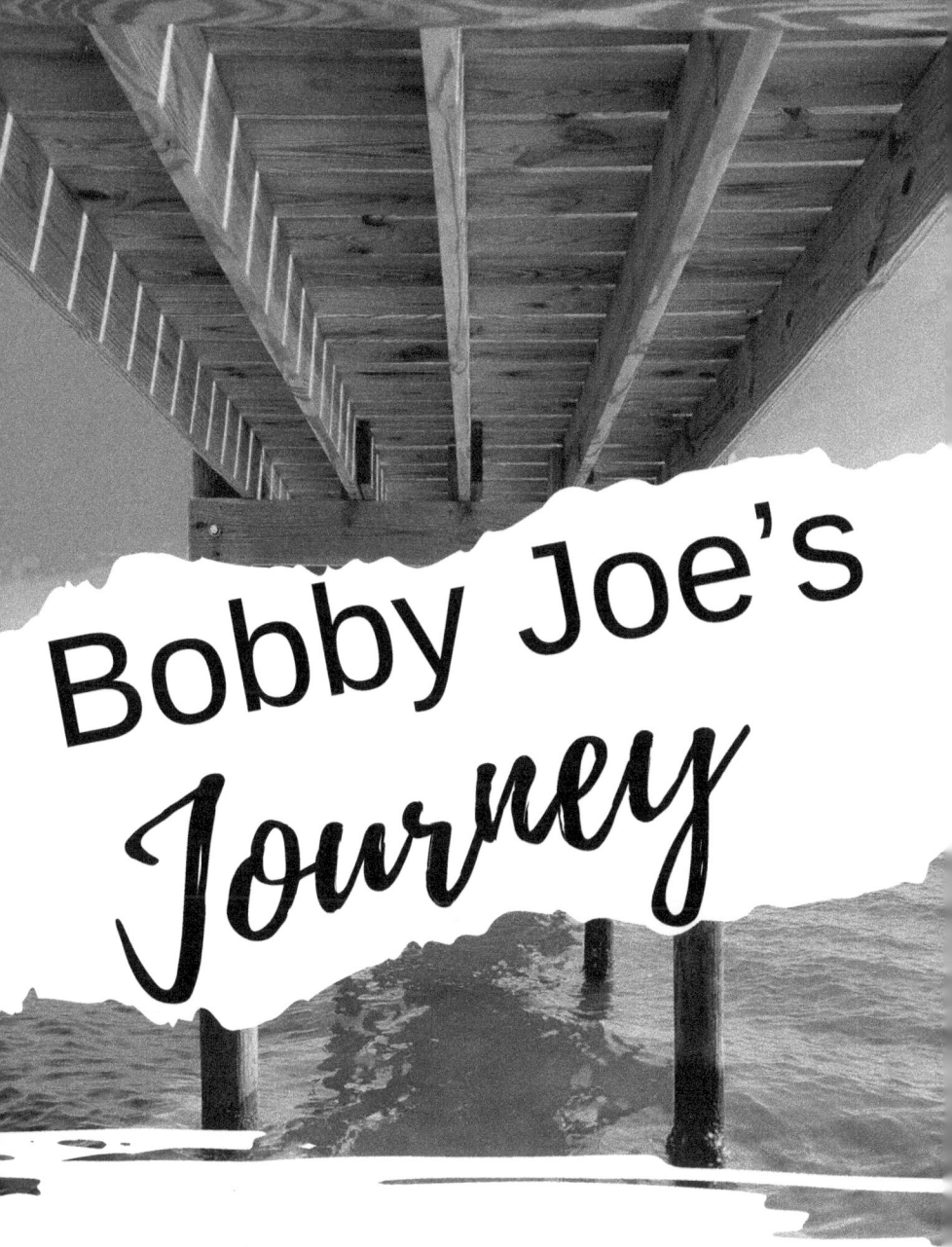

Bobby Joe's Journey

"I am accepted!"

As a child, my family and I lived in a small house in a coastal town in Northwest Florida. During that time, my parents, two siblings, and I suffered the tragedy of a horrible house fire.

I remember the local news station coming out, and doing a story about the fire. It was remarkable how the community responded! We had so many people, including my teacher, who poured out their hearts to us.

The love of Christ was evident, as HE met our needs through our neighbors. They were generous in helping us recover from the devastation. As a child, I experienced His love through their actions.

Later, I had an accident that caused me to suffer a traumatic brain injury. The injury was severe, and had created a learning deficiency. I struggled academically. For children and teens, it's difficult to understand those who are different; it's honestly something that, until recently, was sort of pushed aside.

I believe that in the past, as a society, we've done a poor job of educating students to understand and accept learning diversities. Fortunately, today, there are some educators that understand the importance of raising awareness, and are willing to integrate that understanding within their classrooms.

Through our house fire, I had experienced the love of a community. But unfortunately, through my brain injury, I only experienced the rejection of my peers.

I was bullied.

I felt pushed aside by classmates who were afraid of my differences, due to a lack of understanding them.
I longed for acceptance.

My search for it led me to making unhealthy choices.

My struggles in school, along with the taunts from fellow classmates, increased my lack of self-worth; and led me towards depression.

Not long after, in an attempt to hide my pain, I found myself drinking. A lot. I even dropped out of school.

The path was long, and very lonely. My vision was set on the disappointments I experienced through others. I allowed their words and actions to push me away. For years alcohol stole from me and caused even more pain and heartache.

Until one day I became tired, and I began to look for ways out.

Isn't it funny how when we are at "our end" that with God it's actually "our beginning"?

God intervened and led me to a local non-profit Christian ministry. They provided the needed programs to help me get on my feet.

Through their love and support I was able to find *ACCEPTANCE.*

I found friends.

I found family.

The voids that alcohol were never able to fill were filled through a relationship with Christ.

Ephesians 1:4-8 tells us this:

"He chose us in Him before the foundation of the world, that we should be holy and without blame before him in love, having predestined us to adoption as sons by Jesus Christ to Himself, according to the good pleasure of His will, to the praise of the glory of His grace, by which He made us ACCEPTED in the Beloved. In Him we have redemption through His blood, the forgiveness of sins, according to the riches of His grace which he made to abound toward us in all wisdom and prudence."

I have learned that I am ACCEPTED.

I have learned that I am BELOVED.

When I understood that my self-worth is not found through the acceptance of others, but only through God's love for me, it truly set me FREE.

I've learned that through bad can come good.

Out of pain can come strength.

It begins with a willingness to find the good in the bad, and that begins with a heart of gratitude. If we keep our eyes and mind on the tough circumstances around us, we will *miss* the blessings that are just beyond them.

We have to change our focus!

I've learned the importance of keeping my focus on God. I've learned the importance of believing what HE says about me.

I'm learning how to protect my mind.

I'm learning how to protect my heart.

I'm grateful.

I am who I am... and I am HIS.

"Bear one another's burdens, and so fulfill the law of Christ."
Galatians 6:2

Adrienne's *Journey*

"This is who you are."

I wasn't brought up in church.
I did believe in God as a child, but just about as much as I believed in the Easter bunny or Santa Clause. Even though I don't have very many childhood memories, I do remember feeling shame and loneliness at an early age.

At the age of 14, I attempted suicide. It was the only way I knew to stop the pain I was feeling, and the thoughts that had invaded my mind. After the suicide attempt, a psychiatrist prescribed medications for the depression. But alone, they didn't help.
I hated myself; and in another desperate attempt to find peace from the war in my mind, I began drinking with friends from school.

I felt lost.
I felt unwanted.
I felt unloved.

At the age of nineteen, I met a man who was a few years older than me. He had a two-year-old son. I decided I wanted to pursue a relationship with him; and to become the best mom I could be to his child. It was my attempt to feel normal.

But still, I felt alone.

It was at the age of twenty-two that I said my first honest prayer to God, who I didn't even know; at least, not on a personal level, I just knew "of" him. So, I prayed. I asked for a daughter, and hoped that she would look just like me. I wanted to name her Ella. It was a desire that I had in my heart.

Shortly after praying that prayer, I became pregnant. Sure enough, I gave birth to a beautiful little girl; and I named her Ella. To this day, it's astonishing how much she looks like me.

I married her father, and began working at City Hall. I wanted to be the best wife, the best mother, and the best employee. I wanted to do it all. However, as I tried desperately to reach those goals, I became tired. Along with the unreasonable expectations, came more depression. As I battled the war going on in my mind, the deeper I sunk into mental and physical EXHAUSTION.

In an effort to help, my husband offered me one of his A.D.D. medications and told me it would increase my energy level. Wow, did it!!! I could wake up early, work an eight-hour shift, get the kids from school, take my son to soccer, take my daughter to her dance lessons, volunteer at the school, and prepare meals for my family, all while keeping an immaculate home.

However, it wasn't long before I became addicted. Severely addicted. Not only did the drugs offer a change in energy, but also in behavior. They come as a "strong hold", and they were relentless.

The addiction lasted seven years, until my family couldn't take it any longer, and gave me an ultimatum. Either my husband would leave me, taking our children with him, or I would enter into a rehabilitation center. So, I packed my things, and checked myself in to a thirty-day program. Finally, after getting the drugs out of my system, and thinking I was cured, I thought I had it all figured out.

While in treatment, I had convinced myself that my drug problem had been my husband's fault and before being released, I asked for a divorce.

After my release from the program, I moved in with my parents, and started attending drug rehabilitation group meetings. I worked the required steps. At first, I felt better, but I still had a deep void that couldn't be filled.

And soon, I found myself addicted again.

Only this time, it was to a man.

I had met him during the process of the recovery program. However, instead of recovering, I began to decline. After our marriage, it wasn't long before our relationship became toxic and turbulent. He was emotionally and verbally abusive and had an issue with cheating. His unfaithfulness only added to my lack of self-worth.

Throughout or entire relationship, there was constant infidelity. Yet, when He asked me to marry him, I still said, "Yes." In some way it made me feel wanted.

My decision to marry him broke the heart of my daughter.

However, nothing compared to the pain that I caused her shortly after the wedding. He received the news that he was having a child, by another woman; and found the news to be too much to handle. He relapsed. Before long, I was following down that same dark path with him.

But this time, the drugs I used were much harder and much more dangerous than anything I had ever experienced. After using, I immediately experienced a psychotic break, and lost all touch with reality.

I was absolutely lost... deeper than ever before. My family turned me away, and told me they no longer recognized the person I had become.

I begged for halfway houses to let me in, but my mind was not clear enough to even articulate full sentences. So instead, I was turned away.

I pleaded with police officers, urging them to find a reason to arrest me. Surely there was something, a crime I had committed to warrant an arrest. Instead, they took me to mental hospitals, who would then release me shortly after. The cycle continued.

In addition to my pain, I had also found out that my precious twelve-year old daughter was now aware of my circumstances... that I was addicted to meth, and had lost my mind.

Papers were filed to remove my parental rights temporarily. I had nothing, and no one. I felt as though every ounce of dignity that I once was trying so desperately to hold on to, had been stripped away. I was at the bottom.

Until one night, in the heat of September, I found myself in a dark, and dirty hotel room with an air-conditioner that didn't work. I was afraid, and I was desperate.

There, in that broken down hotel room, I walked up to the bathroom mirror, looked at my ratted hair, tear-streaked face, dingy sweaty t-shirt, and heard a voice. It said to me, "This ISN'T who you are!"

I then saw, in that same mirror, a woman pacing back and forth while lifting her hands in a peculiar manner. As she walked left to right, she began lifting up other women; who then began mimicking the same arm movement. Suddenly, the movements that I was witnessing in the vision, I began to do. Oddly, if felt so natural to me. It was at that moment, I heard that same voice whisper to me, "THIS is who you are. I am Christ, and you are mine."

In that instant, there was a peace and a clarity that came over me as it filled the room. There was a familiarity of the presence of Jesus. I knew at that moment; I would never be the same.

I believed and instantly knew that I was a DAUGHTER. God's daughter. It was a presence that I had never felt before.

It was pure. It was life. My Heavenly Father had just met me right where I was.

This was also my first experience with worship. I wasn't in a church, not bent at an altar, nor was a preacher present. There was not a platform with shining lights, no instruments, no singers, and no praise team. There was only me... and the presence of God.

When I came out of that bathroom, I knew that I would never be the same. I couldn't wait to tell my husband. I wanted to share with him my experience; and together, I wanted us to go and tell his mom.

My mother-in-law attended church regularly, and somehow, I knew she would understand. I couldn't wait to share my experience with her, and talk about the presence I had been in. Even though it was 2:00 am, I didn't hesitate to wake her. I was filled with a supernatural energy and excitement! For the first time, I finally felt ALIVE!

I remember saying to her, "I'm a Christian now! I want to go to church with you in the morning. I know you won't believe me now, but I promise one day you will!"

That morning, she took me to church. I experienced more of the same presence as I had witnessed the night before. There, in that church, I confessed that Jesus was Lord, and I invited Him into my heart, to become my Savior, to cleanse me... and He did.

Later, my husband also gave his heart to God. Unfortunately, he wasn't committed to following Christ, and before long, was backsliding... away from God. As for me, I had tasted of life. I had something I couldn't let go of. So I kept moving forward.

In the past, I had turned to drugs to "get me through", but now I was learning how to depend on God. To trust Him for everything I needed; and I found that He was enough.

I was even willing to serve my husband, even though he was unfaithful.

I learned to lift my hands and worship. I learned to dance, and give God praise. During nights when I knew my husband was being unfaithful, instead of breaking down, I chose to lean on God. I grew in God's Word. It provided me with strength and peace; a strength and peace that drugs were never able to provide.

One of my favorite verses became, "For I consider that the sufferings of this present time are not worth comparing with the glory that is to be revealed to us," (Romans 8:18).
Even though my marriage contained strong holds, something in me, knew that God would make a way for my total Freedom.

Not long after, once again, my husband attempted to follow Christ. And this time, I thought it was different. I thought maybe my marriage would be restored. Instead, he relapsed... again. His pursuit for drugs and his weakness for lust, was much stronger than his pursuit for God.

It became too dangerous to remain in the marriage. So, I made the choice to leave, and with that choice, not only came safety, but also a freedom that I never knew existed. Through the strength that I received, God had parted my sea, and the ground I stepped on was solid.

During that time, God showered me with so much mercy and so much grace. He poured over me an intimate love. Even though the road was long, and sometimes hard, He never abandoned me. He walked me through.

I continued to grow in God's Word, and in understanding His love for me. During that time, He taught me how to serve at church.

Today, I'm still serving, at the same church where I asked the Lord to become my Savior. I'm presently the director of Kid's Church, and God has given me a passion to nurture them. I'm so extremely blessed to have so many spiritual children through this ministry. I also serve on the prayer team, and almost daily, God uses me in a beautiful way.

I'm overwhelmed by His goodness!
Through HIM, I've found JOY and PEACE that are immeasurable! My parents are proud of me. My mother was saved last year, and shortly after, my brother was saved.

I am now, newly married to an amazing man of God. Our marriage is founded on God's design. We both seek Him. There's compassion, friendship, respect, kindness, and above all a shared passion for Jesus. My husband serves as well, through our church worship team.

Together, we're living a life that's full of abundance. God's blessings are GOOD. We own a business, named "Made New", because it's a beautiful reflection of our life, and the promise found in 2 Corinthians 5:17...

"Therefore if anyone be in Christ, he is a NEW CREATION. Old things have passed away, and ALL things become NEW!"

My daughter is now eighteen. We talk occasionally. Even though she isn't ready to have a close relationship with me, I believe one day she will. I'm also praying for her salvation, that one day, she will call on Jesus and invite Him into her heart.

When she does, my testimony will continue; that what once was lost, is found. Restoration is coming. I'm willing to wait. Because God's timing is always perfect.

Eighteen years ago my prayer, for a daughter to name Ella, was answered. God isn't done. I'm believing the promise found in Isaiah 40:31...

"They that wait upon the Lord shall renew their strength, they shall mount up with wings as eagles, they shall run, and not be weary, and they shall walk, and not faint."

It all started in a moment, in a dark bathroom, where at first, I felt alone. But God, in His mercy, met me there.

Christ redeemed me!

His light broke through the darkness, and illuminated what He called me to be... FREE!

For you were once darkness,
but now you are light in the Lord.
Walk as children of light...
Ephesians 5:8

Rick's
Journey

"All I heard was, 'Go Pray'."

My siblings and I were raised on the foundation of Christianity; in a home where faith in God was the norm.

I was two when my dad passed away from a brain tumor. I don't remember much from that period of my life, although I do remember that my mother's faith was the anchor that held us all together. It kept our home steady.

Yet, as a young teen, even with that anchor, I took off in a different direction. I was hungry for what was out in the world. The world was calling to me, and I was listening.

I had a love for music. Any kind of music. I tried several different instruments and soon decided that the drums were my favorite. Playing the drums, quickly became my passion.

My first drum set was cardboard boxes. I would beat on those things every single day. When my mom searched and bought me an actual drum set, it changed my world. I took every single dollar I could earn to pawn shops to buy pieces to add to my set. Before long I had a complete double bass set, and my heart was full; or so I felt.

At fourteen, I was on my way; I just didn't know where I was going. By sixteen I had finally worked up the nerve to tell my mom I no longer wanted to go to church. Her response was not what I was expecting. "Okay," she replied, "I'll just turn you over to God."

Looking back, I thought her reply was simple and easy, but I had no idea how powerful it would be. At that time, I felt free. I was blinded by my passion for music. I wanted to play for anyone, anywhere. I wanted to captivate people with my music. However, I had no idea that I was the one about to be taken captive.

From the age of sixteen to twenty-four I thought I was truly living the life. I was a drummer in both a rock n' roll, and a country band. We played for private events, in bars, and wherever we were invited.

Little did I know that the lifestyle that goes with that scene was about to be in full swing. From the outside it appeared as though I was "living the life". Inside, however, I was slowly dying. Slowly dying in secret.

I had met a woman. Later, we moved in together. She had a daughter and together we had a son out of wedlock. Together we drank and smoked pot. I continued to play drums and party with my fellow band members. For a while, it felt right; but eventually, things began to fall apart.

Due to my own choices I had made a mess of my life. At night, I would lay in bed thinking of ways to take my own life. Even though as a child I had been to church, I had never said a prayer on my own.

Then, one night as I was watching television, while sitting there smoking and drinking, I had an encounter with God. I just didn't completely understand it at the time. I still can't describe the sensation I felt.

I heard a voice. It was clear. It said only two words, "Go pray."

I got up and went to my bedroom. I knelt beside the bed, just like I had seen my mother do. I can still hear the words that came out of my mouth that night...

"God, if you will help me marry this woman I'm living with, give me my son in my name, and change my life, I will serve you the rest of it."

Within six weeks later, we were married. My son had my last name. We had a new home, and I had a new job. I was no longer drinking or smoking, and I attended church whenever I could.

Yet, I continued to play drums in a country band. I wanted the money, but the late-night gigs made it tough to wake up on Sunday mornings.

I remember clearly, coming home early one morning, after playing in a bar all night, that I heard a voice. It was gentle, but clear. It said,
" You can't serve Me and entertain the world."

I knew instantly that God was speaking to me. I went home that morning, packed up my drums, placed them in my closet, and quit. I told my wife about the experience and the decision I had made. She was angry with me.

After my first prayer, asking God to change my life, my habits began to change. However, my wife didn't want to follow in the same direction.

My decision to stop playing and going to bars drew an even deeper trench between us. She wanted that lifestyle, but I was done. Within a month she had filed for divorce, and I moved out.

The remarkable thing is, that the following morning after following God's command and putting away my drums, I went to visit a local church. It was the largest in our area, and I had never visited it before. I noticed that there wasn't anyone on their drum set during worship. After the service my mom mentioned to someone that I was a drummer. The very next Sunday I played the drums there, and I continued for the next eighteen years.

I have been blessed to be a youth pastor, a Chaplain, a prison, and jail minister, and now an author. God can do things we never expected if we are willing to trust and obey Him.

In 2017, I suffered a severe stroke on my brainstem that left me physically disabled. Yet, every time I think about walking away from it all, God quickly reminds me of a particular part of my prayer, "I will serve you the rest of it."

I quickly repent.

Here I am, sixty years old, and I can't imagine life without God. He has been my Savior, my Father, my Peace, and my best friend. When Jesus asked the disciples, "Will you leave also?", Peter responded "Where would we go, You have the words of eternal life."

Jesus came to give life, so that we could not only have eternal life in Heaven, but that while here on earth we can LIVE. In Luke 19, Jesus said these words, "For the Son of Man has come to seek and to save that which was lost."

I was lost, but He sought me. He saved me.

When my Mom spoke those powerful words, "I'll just turn you over to God," His promise, found in Deuteronomy 4:31, was set before me...

"For God is compassionate. The Lord your God won't fail you. He won't destroy you or forget the covenant that He confirmed with your ancestors."

I'm grateful that I didn't listen to the voice of suicide that night. Instead, I heard and responded to the voice of God, who wanted to become my Heavenly Father. His plan and will for our life is always perfect, we just have to be willing to OBEY.

"Make a joyful shout to God, all the earth.
Sing to the glory of His name.
Offer Him glory and praise!"
Psalm 66:1,2

We, at Kainon Land Media,
want you to know
that you are not alone!
The people who so bravely
shared their stories
also want you to know,
YOU ARE NOT ALONE!

"Therefore, having so vast a cloud
of witnesses surrounding us, and
throwing off everything
that hinders us and especially the sin
that so easily entangles us, let us keep
running with ENDURANCE
the race set before us,
fixing our attention on Jesus,
the pioneer and perfecter of the faith,
who, in view of the joy set before Him,
endured the cross, disregarding its
shame, and has sat down
at the right hand
of the throne of God."
Hebrews 12: 1, 2

My Reflections:

_____

_____

_____

_____

_____

_____

_____

_____

_____

*Please use this space to write what The Holy Spirit
spoke to you as you read these Freedom Journeys,
or record the personal thoughts you may want to remember.*

My Reflections continued...

_____

_____

_____

_____

_____

_____

_____

_____

_____

*Please use this space to write what The Holy Spirit
spoke to you as you read these Freedom Journeys,
or record the personal thoughts you may want to remember.*

"Return to your house,
and tell what great things
God has done for you."
Luke 8:39